50
AND
PROUD
OF IT

summersdale

50 AND PROUD OF IT

Summersdale Publishers Ltd
46 West Street
Chichester
West Sussex
PO19 1RP
UK

www.summersdale.com

Printed and bound in the Czech Republic

ISBN: 978-1-84953-563-2

Substantial discounts on bulk quantities of Summersdale books are available to corporations, professional associations and other organisations. For details contact Nicky Douglas by telephone: +44 (0) 1243 756902, fax: +44 (0) 1243 786300 or email: nicky@summersdale.com.

TO...

FROM...

CONTENTS

ANOTHER YEAR OLDER

BY THE TIME WE HIT
50... WE HAVE LEARNED
TO TAKE LIFE SERIOUSLY,
BUT NEVER OURSELVES.

Marie Dressler

WE'RE VINTAGE!

Jennifer Saunders and Dawn French
on both reaching 50

HAPPY TWENTIETH ANNIVERSARY OF YOUR THIRTIETH BIRTHDAY!

Anonymous

IT TAKES A LONG TIME TO BECOME YOUNG.

Pablo Picasso

AS A GRADUATE OF
THE ZSA ZSA GABOR
SCHOOL OF CREATIVE
MATHEMATICS, I
HONESTLY DO NOT KNOW
HOW OLD I AM.

Erma Bombeck

FORTY IS THE OLD AGE
OF YOUTH; 50 THE
YOUTH OF OLD AGE.

Victor Hugo

TO ME, OLD AGE IS ALWAYS 15 YEARS OLDER THAN I AM.

Bernard M. Baruch

ABOUT THE ONLY THING
THAT COMES TO US
WITHOUT EFFORT
IS OLD AGE.

Gloria Pitzer

I'D LIKE TO GROW
VERY OLD AS SLOWLY
AS POSSIBLE.

Charles Lamb

HOW OLD WOULD YOU
BE IF YOU DIDN'T KNOW
HOW OLD YOU WERE?

Satchel Paige

THE WOMAN WHO TELLS
HER AGE IS EITHER
TOO YOUNG TO HAVE
ANYTHING TO LOSE
OR TOO OLD TO HAVE
ANYTHING TO GAIN.

Chinese proverb

I REFUSE TO ADMIT I'M MORE THAN 52, EVEN IF THAT DOES MAKE MY SONS ILLEGITIMATE.

Nancy Astor

FEW WOMEN ADMIT
THEIR AGE. FEW MEN
ACT THEIRS.

Anonymous

NO WOMAN
SHOULD EVER BE
QUITE ACCURATE
ABOUT HER AGE.
IT LOOKS SO
CALCULATING.

Oscar Wilde

FOR ALL THE ADVANCES
IN MEDICINE, THERE IS
STILL NO CURE FOR THE
COMMON BIRTHDAY.

John Glenn

FOR YEARS I WANTED
TO BE OLDER, AND
NOW I AM.

Margaret Atwood

BIRTHDAYS ONLY COME
ONCE A YEAR UNLESS
YOU'RE JOAN COLLINS,
IN WHICH CASE THEY
ONLY COME EVERY
FOUR YEARS.

Steve Bauer

JUST REMEMBER,
ONCE YOU'RE OVER THE
HILL YOU BEGIN TO
PICK UP SPEED.

Charles M. Schulz

JUST
WHAT
I ALWAYS
WANTED

YOUTH IS THE GIFT OF
NATURE, BUT AGE IS A
WORK OF ART.

Garson Kanin

A COMFORTABLE OLD AGE
IS THE REWARD OF A
WELL-SPENT YOUTH.

Maurice Chevalier

YESTERDAY IS HISTORY,
TOMORROW IS A
MYSTERY, BUT TODAY IS
A GIFT. THAT IS WHY
IT IS CALLED THE
PRESENT.

Eleanor Roosevelt ·

A GIFT, WITH A KIND
COUNTENANCE, IS A
DOUBLE PRESENT.

Thomas Fuller

EVERY WRINKLE IS BUT
A NOTCH IN THE QUIET
CALENDAR OF A WELL-
SPENT LIFE.

Charles Dickens

EACH DAY COMES
BEARING ITS OWN GIFTS.
UNTIE THE RIBBONS.

Ruth Ann Schabacker

A TRUE FRIEND REMEMBERS YOUR BIRTHDAY BUT NOT YOUR AGE.

Anonymous

AGE IS JUST A
NUMBER. IT'S TOTALLY
IRRELEVANT UNLESS, OF
COURSE, YOU HAPPEN TO
BE A BOTTLE OF WINE.

Joan Collins

A FRIEND NEVER
DEFENDS A HUSBAND
WHO GETS HIS WIFE AN
ELECTRIC SKILLET FOR
HER BIRTHDAY.

Erma Bombeck

AT MY AGE THE BEST
GIFT ONE CAN HOPE
FOR IS A CONTINUING
SENSE OF HUMOUR.
THE ABILITY TO
LAUGH, ESPECIALLY AT
OURSELVES, KEEPS THE
HEART LIGHT AND THE
MIND YOUNG.

Anonymous

NO ONE IS SO OLD AS TO
THINK HE CANNOT LIVE
ONE MORE YEAR.

Cicero

BIRTHDAYS ARE GOOD
FOR YOU. STATISTICS
SHOW THAT THE PEOPLE
WHO HAVE THE MOST
LIVE THE LONGEST.

Larry Lorenzoni

THERE ARE 364 DAYS
WHEN YOU MIGHT GET
UN-BIRTHDAY PRESENTS
... AND ONLY ONE FOR
BIRTHDAY PRESENTS,
YOU KNOW.

Lewis Carroll

YOU KNOW YOU'RE
GETTING OLD WHEN THE
ONLY THING YOU WANT
FOR YOUR BIRTHDAY
IS NOT TO BE
REMINDED OF IT.

Anonymous

GROWING OLD IS
MANDATORY; GROWING
UP IS OPTIONAL.

Chili Davis

GRIN
AND
BEAR
IT

IF I'D KNOWN I WAS
GOING TO LIVE THIS
LONG, I'D HAVE TAKEN
BETTER CARE OF
MYSELF.

Eubie Blake

IF YOU FIND YOURSELF
50 YEARS OLD AND YOU
AREN'T DOING WHAT YOU
LOVE, THEN WHAT'S
THE POINT?

Jim Carrey

WHENEVER THE TALK
TURNS TO AGE, I SAY I
AM 49 PLUS VAT.

Lionel Blair

THE YEARS TEACH MUCH WHICH THE DAYS NEVER KNEW.

Ralph Waldo Emerson

ANOTHER BELIEF OF
MINE: THAT EVERYONE
ELSE MY AGE IS AN
ADULT, WHEREAS I AM
MERELY IN DISGUISE.

Margaret Atwood

PERHAPS ONE HAS TO BE
VERY OLD BEFORE ONE
LEARNS TO BE AMUSED
RATHER THAN SHOCKED.

Pearl S. Buck

NICE TO BE HERE? AT MY AGE IT'S NICE TO BE ANYWHERE.

George Burns

AGEING IS NOT 'LOST YOUTH' BUT A NEW STAGE OF OPPORTUNITY AND STRENGTH.

Betty Friedan

IT IS A MISTAKE TO
REGARD AGE AS A
DOWNHILL GRADE
TOWARD DISSOLUTION.
THE REVERSE IS TRUE.
AS ONE GROWS OLDER,
ONE CLIMBS WITH
SURPRISING STRIDES.

George Sand

I'M LIKE OLD WINE. THEY
DON'T BRING ME OUT
VERY OFTEN, BUT I'M
WELL PRESERVED.

Rose Kennedy

I BELIEVE IN LOYALTY;
I THINK WHEN A WOMAN
REACHES AN AGE SHE
LIKES SHE SHOULD
STICK TO IT.

Eva Gabor

AGE IS SOMETHING
THAT DOESN'T MATTER,
UNLESS YOU ARE
A CHEESE.

Billie Burke

MY MOTHER IS GOING
TO HAVE TO STOP LYING
ABOUT HER AGE BECAUSE
PRETTY SOON I'M GOING
TO BE OLDER THAN
SHE IS.

Tripp Evans

ZEAL, N.: A CERTAIN
NERVOUS DISORDER
AFFLICTING THE YOUNG
AND INEXPERIENCED.

Ambrose Bierce

THERE IS ONLY ONE
CURE FOR GREY HAIR.
IT WAS INVENTED BY
A FRENCHMAN. IT IS
CALLED THE GUILLOTINE.

P. G. Wodehouse

DO A LITTLE DANCE, MAKE A LITTLE LOVE

OLD PEOPLE AREN'T
EXEMPT FROM HAVING
FUN AND DANCING...
AND PLAYING.

Liz Smith

THERE'S A KIND OF
CONFIDENCE THAT COMES
WHEN YOU'RE IN YOUR
FORTIES AND FIFTIES,
AND MEN FIND THAT
INCREDIBLY ATTRACTIVE.

Peggy Northrop

MIDDLE AGE IS HAVING
A CHOICE BETWEEN
TWO TEMPTATIONS AND
CHOOSING THE ONE
THAT'LL GET YOU
HOME EARLIER.

Dan Bennett

IT'S SEX, NOT YOUTH,
THAT'S WASTED ON
THE YOUNG.

Janet Harris

ONE OF THE SIGNS
OF PASSING YOUTH IS
THE BIRTH OF A SENSE
OF FELLOWSHIP WITH
OTHER HUMAN BEINGS
AS WE TAKE OUR PLACE
AMONG THEM.

Virginia Woolf

YOU KNOW YOU'RE
KNOCKING ON WHEN
YOU FEEL LIKE THE
MORNING-AFTER-
THE-NIGHT-BEFORE
WITHOUT HAVING BEEN
ANYWHERE.

Anonymous

THE YOUNG SOW
WILD OATS. THE OLD
GROW SAGE.

Winston Churchill

I'LL KEEP
SWIVELLING
MY HIPS UNTIL
THEY NEED
REPLACING.

Tom Jones

I'M LIMITLESS AS FAR
AS AGE IS CONCERNED...
AS LONG AS HE HAS A
DRIVER'S LICENCE.

Kim Cattrall
on dating younger men

OLD WOOD BEST TO BURN,
OLD WINE TO DRINK, OLD
FRIENDS TO TRUST, AND
OLD AUTHORS TO READ.

Francis Bacon

A MAN IS A FOOL IF
HE DRINKS BEFORE
HE REACHES 50, AND
A FOOL IF HE DOESN'T
DRINK AFTERWARD.

Frank Lloyd Wright

WE'VE BOTH HIT 50,
AND WE CELEBRATE IT.
THERE IS NO DOOMY
SIDE TO IT... WE'RE
NEARLY GROWN-UP NOW,
BUT NOT QUITE.

Dawn French and Jennifer Saunders

MAY YOU LIVE ALL THE
DAYS OF YOUR LIFE.

Jonathan Swift

IF YOU THINK HITTING
40 IS LIBERATING, WAIT
TILL YOU HIT 50.

Michelle Pfeiffer

YOUNG
AT
HEART

YOU CAN'T TURN BACK
THE CLOCK, BUT YOU CAN
WIND IT UP AGAIN.

Bonnie Prudden

THE GREAT THING ABOUT
GETTING OLDER IS THAT
YOU DON'T LOSE ALL
THE OTHER AGES
YOU'VE BEEN.

Madeleine L'Engle

THE OLD BELIEVE
EVERYTHING; THE
MIDDLE-AGED SUSPECT
EVERYTHING:
THE YOUNG KNOW
EVERYTHING.

Oscar Wilde

CHILDREN ARE A GREAT
COMFORT IN YOUR
OLD AGE — AND THEY
HELP YOU REACH IT
FASTER, TOO.

Lionel Kauffman

A YOUNG MAN IS
EMBARRASSED TO
QUESTION AN
OLDER ONE.

Homer

GROWING OLD IS A BAD
HABIT WHICH A BUSY
MAN HAS NO TIME
TO FORM.

André Maurois

I'M SURPRISED THAT I'M
50... I STILL FEEL
LIKE A KID.

Bruce Willis

WHEN GRACE IS JOINED
WITH WRINKLES, IT IS
ADORABLE. THERE IS AN
UNSPEAKABLE DAWN IN
HAPPY OLD AGE.

Victor Hugo

WITH AGE COMES THE
INNER, THE HIGHER
LIFE. WHO WOULD BE
FOREVER YOUNG, TO
DWELL ALWAYS IN
EXTERNALS?

Elizabeth Cady Stanton

AS IS A TALE, SO IS LIFE:
NOT HOW LONG IT IS,
BUT HOW GOOD IT IS, IS
WHAT MATTERS.

Seneca

A MAN IS NOT OLD AS LONG AS HE IS SEEKING SOMETHING.

Jean Rostand

ONE OF THE BEST PARTS
OF GROWING OLDER?
YOU CAN FLIRT ALL
YOU LIKE SINCE YOU'VE
BECOME HARMLESS.

Liz Smith

TO KEEP THE HEART
UNWRINKLED, TO BE
HOPEFUL, KINDLY,
CHEERFUL, REVERENT
– THAT IS TO TRIUMPH
OVER OLD AGE.

Thomas Bailey Aldrich

OLDER AND WISER?

IF YOU CARRY YOUR
CHILDHOOD WITH YOU,
YOU NEVER BECOME
OLDER.

Tom Stoppard

TO KNOW HOW TO GROW
OLD IS THE MASTERWORK
OF WISDOM.

Henri-Frédéric Amiel

NONE ARE SO OLD
AS THOSE WHO HAVE
OUTLIVED ENTHUSIASM.

Henry David Thoreau

OLD MEN ARE FOND OF
GIVING GOOD ADVICE, TO
CONSOLE THEMSELVES
FOR BEING NO LONGER
IN A POSITION TO GIVE
BAD EXAMPLES.

François de La Rochefoucauld

YOUNG MEN'S MINDS ARE
ALWAYS CHANGEABLE,
BUT WHEN AN OLD MAN
IS CONCERNED IN A
MATTER, HE LOOKS BOTH
BEFORE AND AFTER.

Homer

THE BEST WAY TO GET
MOST HUSBANDS TO
DO SOMETHING IS TO
SUGGEST THAT PERHAPS
THEY'RE TOO OLD
TO DO IT.

Anne Bancroft

THE AGEING PROCESS
HAS YOU FIRMLY IN ITS
GRASP IF YOU NEVER
GET THE URGE TO
THROW A SNOWBALL.

Doug Larson

LOVE HAS MORE DEPTH
AS YOU GET OLDER.

Kirk Douglas

OLD AGE PUTS MORE WRINKLES IN OUR MINDS THAN ON OUR FACES.

Michel de Montaigne

YOU ARE ONLY YOUNG
ONCE, BUT YOU CAN BE
IMMATURE FOR
A LIFETIME.

John P. Grier

HE'S SO OLD THAT WHEN
HE ORDERS A THREE-
MINUTE EGG, THEY
ASK FOR THE MONEY
UP FRONT.

Milton Berle

I HAVE ENJOYED
GREATLY THE SECOND
BLOOMING... SUDDENLY
YOU FIND – AT THE AGE
OF 50, SAY – THAT A
WHOLE NEW LIFE HAS
OPENED BEFORE YOU.

Agatha Christie

BECOMING A
GRANDMOTHER IS
WONDERFUL. ONE
MOMENT YOU'RE JUST
A MOTHER. THE NEXT
YOU ARE ALL-WISE AND
PREHISTORIC.

Pam Brown

THE SURPRISING THING
ABOUT YOUNG FOOLS IS
HOW MANY SURVIVE TO
BECOME OLD FOOLS.

Doug Larson

NO MAN IS EVER OLD
ENOUGH TO KNOW
BETTER.

Holbrook Jackson

BEFORE YOU CONTRADICT
AN OLD MAN, MY FAIR
FRIEND, YOU SHOULD
ENDEAVOUR TO
UNDERSTAND HIM.

George Santayana

WHEN I WAS A BOY OF
14, MY FATHER WAS
SO IGNORANT I COULD
HARDLY STAND TO HAVE
THE OLD MAN AROUND.
BUT WHEN I GOT TO 21, I
WAS ASTONISHED AT HOW
MUCH HE HAD LEARNED
IN SEVEN YEARS.

Mark Twain

I'M AIMING BY THE TIME
I'M 50 TO STOP BEING
AN ADOLESCENT.

Wendy Cope

LIVE, LOVE AND LAST

NO MAN LOVES LIFE
LIKE HIM THAT'S
GROWING OLD.

Sophocles

NOBODY GROWS OLD
MERELY BY LIVING A
NUMBER OF YEARS. WE
GROW OLD BY DESERTING
OUR IDEALS.

Samuel Ullman

I DON'T BELIEVE IN
AGEING. I BELIEVE IN
FOREVER ALTERING
ONE'S ASPECT TO
THE SUN.

Virginia Woolf

THE FOLLIES WHICH A
MAN REGRETS MOST IN
HIS LIFE ARE THOSE
WHICH HE DIDN'T
COMMIT WHEN HE HAD
THE OPPORTUNITY.

Helen Rowland

TO STOP AGEING, KEEP
ON RAGING.

Michael Forbes

NO MATTER HOW OLD YOU
ARE, THERE'S ALWAYS
SOMETHING GOOD TO
LOOK FORWARD TO.

Lynn Johnston

THE OTHER DAY A MAN
ASKED ME WHAT I
THOUGHT WAS THE BEST
TIME OF LIFE. 'WHY,' I
ANSWERED, 'NOW.'

David Grayson

MIDDLE AGE IS WHEN WE
CAN DO JUST AS MUCH
AS EVER – BUT WOULD
RATHER NOT.

Anonymous

TOMORROW'S GONE – WE'LL HAVE TONIGHT!

Dorothy Parker

YEARS MAY WRINKLE
THE SKIN, BUT TO
GIVE UP ENTHUSIASM
WRINKLES THE SOUL.

Samuel Ullman

THE TIME TO BEGIN
MOST THINGS IS TEN
YEARS AGO.

Mignon McLaughlin

YOU CAN LIVE TO BE A
HUNDRED IF YOU GIVE
UP ALL THE THINGS
THAT MAKE YOU WANT TO
LIVE TO BE A HUNDRED.

Woody Allen

HE WHO LAUGHS,
LASTS!

Mary Pettibone Poole

THE PURPOSE OF LIFE IS TO FIGHT MATURITY.

Dick Werthimer

AGE DOES NOT PROTECT
YOU FROM LOVE.
BUT LOVE TO SOME
EXTENT, PROTECTS YOU
FROM AGE.

Jeanne Moreau

THE AVERAGE CHILD
LAUGHS ABOUT 400
TIMES PER DAY, THE
AVERAGE ADULT LAUGHS
ONLY 15 TIMES PER DAY.
WHAT HAPPENED TO THE
OTHER 385 LAUGHS?
LAUGH AND LIVE!

Anonymous

ILLS,
PILLS
AND
TWINGES

TIME DOTH FLIT;
OH SHIT!

Dorothy Parker

OLD MINDS ARE LIKE
OLD HORSES; YOU MUST
EXERCISE THEM IF YOU
WISH TO KEEP THEM IN
WORKING ORDER.

John Quincy Adams

MY DOCTOR TOLD ME
TO DO SOMETHING
THAT PUTS ME OUT OF
BREATH, SO I'VE TAKEN
UP SMOKING AGAIN.

Jo Brand

YOU KNOW YOU'VE
REACHED MIDDLE-
AGE WHEN YOUR
WEIGHTLIFTING
CONSISTS MERELY OF
STANDING UP.

Bob Hope

MIDDLE AGE IS WHEN
YOU CHOOSE YOUR
CEREAL FOR THE FIBRE,
NOT THE TOY.

Anonymous

THE YEARS BETWEEN
50 AND 70 ARE THE
HARDEST. YOU ARE
ALWAYS BEING ASKED
TO DO MORE, AND YOU
ARE NOT YET DECREPIT
ENOUGH TO TURN
THEM DOWN.

T. S. Eliot

I WOULD RATHER
BE ROUND AND
JOLLY THAN
THIN AND CROSS.

Ann Widdecombe

I FEEL STRONGER NOW THAN, MAYBE, 20 YEARS AGO. IF YOUR MIND IS STRONG, YOUR BODY WILL BE STRONG.

Madonna

MIDDLE AGE IS THE TIME
WHEN A MAN IS ALWAYS
THINKING IN A WEEK OR
TWO HE WILL FEEL AS
GOOD AS EVER.

Don Marquis

TO GET BACK MY YOUTH
I WOULD DO ANYTHING
IN THE WORLD, EXCEPT
TAKE EXERCISE, GET
UP EARLY, OR BE
RESPECTABLE.

Oscar Wilde

I DON'T FEEL OLD. I
DON'T FEEL ANYTHING
TILL NOON. THAT'S WHEN
IT'S TIME FOR MY NAP.

Bob Hope

I NEVER WORRY ABOUT DIETS. THE ONLY CARROTS THAT INTEREST ME ARE THE NUMBER YOU GET IN A DIAMOND.

Mae West

OLD AGE IS NO PLACE FOR SISSIES.

Bette Davis

AS YOU GET OLDER
THREE THINGS HAPPEN.
THE FIRST IS YOUR
MEMORY GOES, AND I
CAN'T REMEMBER THE
OTHER TWO...

Norman Wisdom

AGE SELDOM ARRIVES
SMOOTHLY OR QUICKLY.
IT'S MORE OFTEN A
SUCCESSION OF JERKS.

Jean Rhys

WHAT MOST PERSONS
CONSIDER AS VIRTUE,
AFTER THE AGE OF
40 IS SIMPLY A LOSS
OF ENERGY.

Voltaire

PEOPLE WHO SAY YOU'RE
JUST AS OLD AS YOU
FEEL ARE ALL WRONG,
FORTUNATELY.

Russell Baker

CHIN UP, CHEST OUT

YOU CAN ONLY PERCEIVE
REAL BEAUTY IN A
PERSON AS THEY
GET OLDER.

Anouk Aimée

MIDDLE AGE IS WHEN
YOUR AGE STARTS
TO SHOW AROUND
YOUR MIDDLE.

Bob Hope

THE AGE OF A WOMAN
DOESN'T MEAN A THING.
THE BEST TUNES ARE
PLAYED ON THE OLDEST
FIDDLES.

Ralph Waldo Emerson

GOOD CHEEKBONES ARE
THE BRASSIERE OF
OLD AGE.

Barbara de Portago

I DON'T PLAN TO GROW
OLD GRACEFULLY; I PLAN
TO HAVE FACELIFTS
UNTIL MY EARS MEET.

Rita Rudner

YOU KNOW YOU'RE
GETTING OLD WHEN YOU
STOP TO TIE YOUR SHOES
AND WONDER WHAT
ELSE YOU CAN DO WHILE
YOU'RE DOWN THERE.

George Burns

ANYONE WHO KEEPS THE
ABILITY TO SEE BEAUTY
NEVER GROWS OLD.

Franz Kafka

PLEASE DON'T RETOUCH MY WRINKLES. IT TOOK ME SO LONG TO EARN THEM.

Anna Magnani

WHEN IT COMES TO
STAYING YOUNG, A MIND-
LIFT BEATS A FACELIFT
ANY DAY.

Marty Bucella

THE LONGER I LIVE
THE MORE BEAUTIFUL
LIFE BECOMES.

Frank Lloyd Wright

ONE OF THE MANY
THINGS NOBODY EVER
TELLS YOU ABOUT
MIDDLE AGE IS THAT IT'S
SUCH A NICE CHANGE
FROM BEING YOUNG.

Dorothy Canfield Fisher

I'M NOT DENYING MY
AGE, I'M EMBELLISHING
MY YOUTH.

Tamara Reynolds

LET US RESPECT GREY
HAIRS, ESPECIALLY
OUR OWN.

J. P. Sears

NATURE GIVES YOU THE
FACE YOU HAVE AT 20,
BUT IT'S UP TO YOU TO
MERIT THE FACE YOU
HAVE AT 50.

Coco Chanel

SHE WAS A
HANDSOME
WOMAN OF 45
AND WOULD
REMAIN SO FOR
MANY YEARS.

Anita Brookner

THE SECRET OF STAYING
YOUNG IS TO LIVE
HONESTLY, EAT SLOWLY
AND LIE ABOUT
YOUR AGE.

Lucille Ball

IT IS NOT HOW OLD
YOU ARE, BUT HOW
YOU ARE OLD.

Marie Dressler

I'VE ONLY GOT ONE WRINKLE AND I'M SITTING ON IT.

Jeanne Calment

THERE IS NO OLD AGE.
THERE IS, AS THERE
ALWAYS WAS, JUST YOU.

Carol Matthau

@EsmeTheBird

If you're interested in finding out more about our books, find us on Facebook at **Summersdale Publishers** and follow us on Twitter at **@Summersdale**.

www.summersdale.com